The ABC Devotional Book

Written by
Rachel Haller Kelley
and
Jill Slusser

Illustrated by
Bettie Haller

Christian Books and Games
P.O. Box 99
Pulaski, Tennessee 38478
www.ChristianBooksandGames.com

Text Copyright ©2011 by Rachel Haller Kelley
and
Jill Slusser
Illustrations Copyright ©2011 by Bettie Haller

Scripture taken from the New King James Version®.
Copyright ©1982 by Thomas Nelson, Inc. Used by permission.

Scriptures taken from the Holy Bible, New International Version®, NIV®.
Copyright ©1973, 1978, 1984, 2011 by Biblica, Inc.™
Used by permission of Zondervan. All rights reserved worldwide.
www.zondervan.com
The "NIV" and "New International Version" are trademarks
registered in the United States Patent and Trademark Office by Biblica, Inc.™

Also quoted: The King James Version (KJV)

All rights reserved including the right of reproduction in whole
or in part in any form.

The text of this book is set in Kristen ITC.
The illustrations are created in Adobe Illustrator.

The ABC Devotional Book/ by Rachel Haller Kelley and Jill Slusser;
Illustrated by Bettie Haller
Summary: The ABC Devotional Book is a fun, kid-friendly book
written to help children understand BIG truths about God
in a very personal way. Each letter of the alphabet,
from A to Z, has a corresponding memory verse for the
child and a short devotional based on the verse.
It also contains easy-to-understand discussion
questions for kids and parents.
ISBN: 978-1-466-21842-0

To Mom who read the Bible to me every morning before school.
— R. K.

*To my mom, Carol Helling, who planted the Word in my heart,
and to my family, Scott, Harrison, Ellanora, Sophia, and Isabella.
This book was written with II Timothy 3:14-17 in mind.*
— J.S.

*"But as for you, continue in what you have learned and have
become convinced of, because you know those from whom
you learned it, and how from infancy you have known
the Holy Scriptures, which are able to make you
wise for salvation through faith in Christ Jesus.
All Scripture is God-breathed and is useful for
teaching, rebuking, correcting and training
in righteousness, so that the servant of God
may be thoroughly equipped for every good work."*
— II Timothy 3:14-17

A

"All we like sheep have gone astray."
Isaiah 53:6

Have you ever been around sheep? They are fairly helpless animals. Sheep wander aimlessly and often get lost.
God says that we are like sheep, but Jesus, our Shepherd, will lead us to heaven if we believe in Him.

Prayer: Lord Jesus, thank you for being my shepherd. Keep me on the right path all the days of my life. Amen.

B

"Be ye kind to one another."
Ephesians 4:32

Today at the playground a friend called you a name that hurt your feelings. Do you call your friend a name back? Or do you say something kind and walk away?
The Bible says God wants us to be kind to one another.

Prayer: Lord, please help me be kind to my family and my friends in words and in actions. In Jesus' name, Amen.

"Children, obey your parents in the Lord for this is right." Ephesians 6:1

You are having so much fun playing when your mom and dad tell you it is time to go to bed. Do you obey and get ready for bed? Or do you ignore them and continue to play? The Bible says that we are to obey our parents.

Prayer: Lord, please help me to obey my parents today and everyday. In Jesus' name, Amen.

C

D

"Draw near to God, and He will draw near to you." James 4:8

Open your Bible and read it or have someone read it to you. What did you learn? Pray to God. Talk to Him about everything. These are two ways you can be close to God. Can you think of other ways?

Prayer: Lord, help me draw near to you. I want to be close to you today, tomorrow, and forever. In Jesus' name, Amen.

"Every good and perfect gift is from above." James 1:17

The Lord gives good and perfect gifts because He is good and perfect. Some of these gifts are family, friends, talents, sunshine, flowers, puppies, kittens, and good food to eat. What gifts has He given to you?

Prayer: Lord, help me to be thankful for every good and perfect gift. I know these gifts come from you. Amen.

F

"For God so loved the world that He gave His only begotten Son, that whosoever believeth in Him should not perish but have everlasting life."   John 3:16

Think of your favorite toy. Is it a train set or some dress-up clothes? Would it be hard for you to give your favorite things away? God gave the ultimate Gift to us — His Son. He gave this Gift because He loves us so much. The Bible says that God sent His Son to die for us so that we can live forever in heaven if we believe in Him.

Prayer: Lord, thank You for sending Your Son so that I might live with You forever. Amen.

"God is love." I John 4:8

Have you ever had a day when you felt like nothing was going right? Your Mom got upset because you spilled a drink on the new carpet. Your Dad got mad when you dropped the phone in the toilet. Your friend didn't play with you at recess. No matter what your day was like, God loves you.
He loves you all the time.

Prayer: Lord, thank you for being a loving God. Amen.

G

"He maketh me to lie down in green pastures, he leadeth me beside the still waters." Psalm 23:2

Do you love to snuggle under the covers in your bed with a soft pillow for your head and a silky blanket in your hand?
You could sleep on the kitchen floor, but that wouldn't be comfortable or cozy.
God loves you more than you can imagine, and He loves taking care of you, too.

Prayer: Thank you for loving me and taking good care of me. Amen.

"I can do all things through Christ who strengthens me."   Phillipians 4:13

Have you ever wanted to do the right thing but were too nervous to do it? Isn't it great to know that God can give you strength when you need it?

Prayer: Lord, thank you that I can do all things through Christ who strenthens me. Amen.

Jesus said to him, "I am the way, the truth, and the life." John 14:6

Some people think there are other ways to get to heaven besides believing in Jesus, but God tells us that believing in his Son is the only way.

Prayer: Thank you, Lord, for showing me how to get to heaven. Help me to be bold enough to tell others that You are the only way. In Jesus' name, Amen.

K

"Keep me as the apple of Your eye."
Psalm 17:8

Look in the mirror at the black circle in the center of your eye. That's your PUPIL, and that's what makes you see.
A long time ago people thought that that black circle was shaped like an apple, and they called it the "apple of your eye." Because that's what helps you see, you protect it and treat it as something precious. The Bible says God keeps us as the apple of His eye, which means we are sooooo special.

Prayer: Lord, thank you for keeping me as the apple of Your eye. Amen.

"Let your light so shine before men, that they may see your good works, and glorify your Father which is in heaven."
Matthew 5:16

Can your friends tell that you're a Christian? Do you play with the child that others may not like? Have you ever invited a friend to your Sunday school class? The Bible tells us to live in such a way that others can tell we are Christians. Then they will want to live for God, too.

Prayer: Lord, help me live for you so that others will want to be Christians.
In Jesus' name, Amen.

L

M

"Make a joyful noise unto the Lord."
Psalm 100:1

Do you think it's fun to make noise?
Do you like to sing or play an instrument?
God likes it when we make a joyful
noise unto Him. Isn't that a good reason
to sing a song or bang on a drum?

Prayer: Lord, help me make a joyful
noise unto You. In Jesus' name, Amen.

N

"No one can serve two masters. Either you will hate the one and love the other, or you will be devoted to the one and despise the other. You cannot serve God and money."

Matthew 6:24

"I want. I want. I want."
Do you hear yourself saying that often?
God wants to be more important to you than money and the things money can buy.

Prayer: Lord, I want You to be more important than anything else in my life. Amen.

O

"O God, you are my God; early will I seek you." Psalm 63:1

Do you feel rested and energetic in the morning? If so, doesn't that make mornings a great time to pray and read your Bible? Spending time with God is a wonderful way to start your day.

Prayer: Lord, help me to start my days with You. In Jesus' name, Amen.

"Put on the whole armour of God."
Ephesians 6:11

Your mom uses a hotpad to protect her hands from getting burned when she takes a pan of cookies from the oven.
In the same way, God gives us what we need to protect ourselves from things in this world that might harm us.

Prayer: Today, Lord, I want to put on the whole armour of God. Amen.

P

"Quench not the Spirit."
I Thessalonians 5:19

Quench: To decrease a thirst or to blow out a flame.

Do you act Christlike? The Lord wants you to be like Him in your words and actions. When you do what you know is wrong, you quench or blow out the Spirit of God, who is telling you the right thing to do.

Prayer: Lord, help me to do the right thing so that others will see You in me. In Jesus name, Amen.

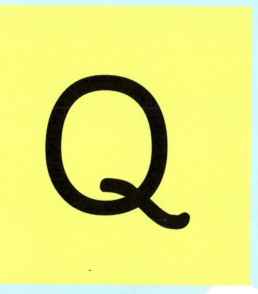

R

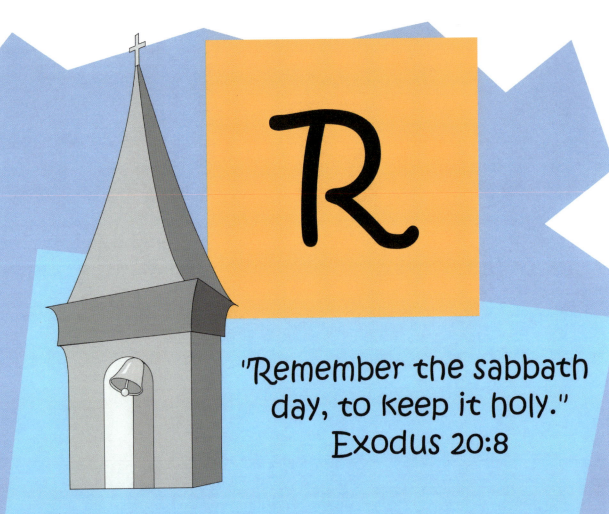

"Remember the sabbath day, to keep it holy."
Exodus 20:8

It's Sunday morning, and you feel tired. Do you get up and go to church? Or do you go back to sleep? Why do you think God wants you to go to church?

Prayer: Lord, help me to remember the sabbath day, and help me to keep it holy. In Jesus' name, Amen.

S

"Sing unto the Lord, bless his name."
Psalm 96:2

Do you like singing the song "Jesus Loves Me?" Sing it now! The Bible tells us to sing to the Lord and to bless His name.

Prayer: Thank you that I can use my voice to praise You. Amen.

"Trust in the Lord with all your heart."
                    Proverbs 3:5

Trust: Depend on

You wake up in the middle of the night, and you feel sick. Do you trust that your parents will make you feel better? Will they get you a drink? Will they give you a hug? Can you depend on them? Of course you can. In the same way you trust in your parents, you can also trust in the Lord.

Prayer: Lord Jesus, help me to trust in You with all my heart, mind, and soul. Amen.

T

"Unto us a Child is born, unto us a Son is given." Isaiah 9:6

A long time ago Jesus left heaven and came to earth as a baby. He is what Christmas is all about. Exchanging gifts at Christmas is fun, but we must always remember that the greatest gift is Jesus Christ.

Prayer: Thank you God for sending us Jesus, the greatest Gift of all. Amen.

"Verily, verily I say unto you, He that believeth on me hath everlasting life." John 6:47

Have you ever wondered what heaven is like? Would it be fun to walk on streets of gold? Do you think heaven will have colors you've never seen before? What would it be like to meet Jesus or talk to an angel? If you could do that, wouldn't it be fun?
Guess what. If you believe in Jesus, you WILL see heaven some day!

Prayer: Thank you, Lord, for the promise of an exciting eternity with You. Amen.

V

"Wait on the Lord." Psalm 27:14

Have you ever wanted a cookie before dinner, and your mom and dad told you that you would have to wait until after you ate? It's hard to wait patiently for things that we want. God wants us to wait on Him. His timing is not our timing, and sometimes that's hard to understand. Are you willing to wait on the Lord?

Prayer: Lord, help me to be patient and to wait on You. In Jesus' name, Amen.

"E**X**cept ye be converted, and become as little children, ye shall not enter into the kingdom of heaven." Matthew 18:3

Have you learned to ride your bike without training wheels yet? Was your mom or dad there for you when the bike tipped from side to side? Just as your childlike faith helped you trust your parents, God wants you to use that same faith to believe and trust in Him.

Prayer: Lord, let me always have a childlike faith so that one day I may enter into the kingdom of heaven. In Jesus' name, Amen.

"You are my friends if you do whatever I command you." John 15:14

Jesus expects us to follow His rules. Do your parents have rules you have to follow? When we follow Jesus' rules or commandments, He calls us His friends. Isn't it neat to know you can be friends with Jesus?

Prayer: Lord, help me to do as You command so that You and I will be friends. In Jesus' name, Amen.

"Zaccheus, make haste and come down, for today I must stay at your house." Luke 19:5

Zaccheus was a short man who made a big effort to see Jesus by climbing a tall tree. He had few friends because he was a tax collector who took more money from people than he should have. Jesus told Zaccheus to come down from the tree so they could visit at his house. Jesus showed love to someone others didn't like, and we should do likewise.

Prayer: Lord, I want to be like you and love others the way You do. Amen.